THE
LUCKY
FEATHER

Captain Castor had been a pirate,
but now he had a job driving a bus.
    He still wore his pirate's clothes.
He had a black jacket and gold earrings
and a red hat with a feather in it.
The feather was from a yellow parrot.
Captain Castor wore it for luck.

Every morning, he put on his hat and sang,
"Day and night, night and day,
my feather keeps bad luck away."
   As he got on his bus, he sang,
"Never, never, no, not ever
will I drive without my feather."

But one day,
Captain Castor lost his feather.
A strong wind tugged it out of his hat,
and it flew away like a yellow arrow.
    "Gone!" cried Captain Castor.
"Gone!" cried all the passengers.
    Captain Castor sat on the steps of
the bus and moaned deep moans.

"Time to go," said the passengers.
"No, no, we cannot go!"
Captain Castor replied.
"Without my feather,
we'll have a dreadful accident."
"But we'll be late!"
said the passengers.
"Better to be late than dead on time,"
said Captain Castor.

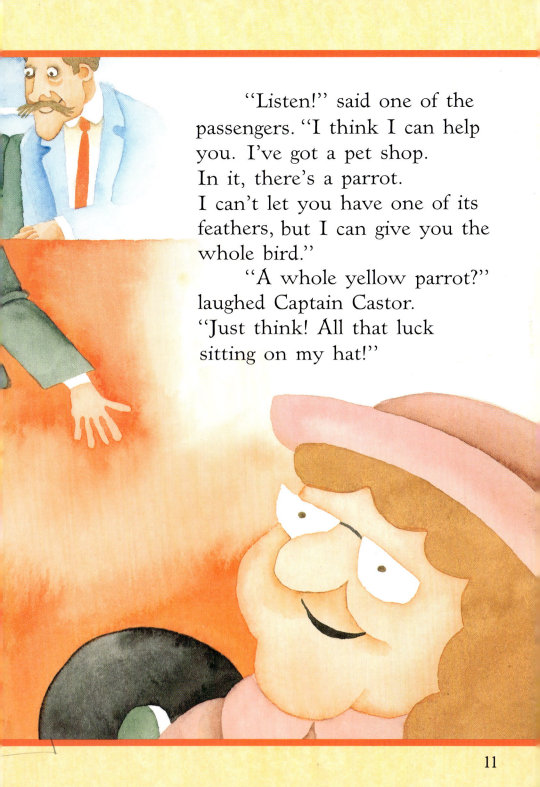

"Listen!" said one of the
passengers. "I think I can help
you. I've got a pet shop.
In it, there's a parrot.
I can't let you have one of its
feathers, but I can give you the
whole bird."

"A whole yellow parrot?"
laughed Captain Castor.
"Just think! All that luck
sitting on my hat!"

"There's one catch,"
said the passenger.
"To get the parrot,
you must drive your bus
to my pet shop."
Captain Castor stopped laughing.
As he got on his bus,
he groaned deep groans.
How could he drive
without a good-luck feather?
"Accident!" he groaned,
starting the engine.
"Accident!" he moaned,
all the way down the road.

But he didn't have an accident.
He drove very well.
He stopped the bus by the pet shop.
The passenger got out
and came back with the yellow parrot.
Sure enough,
it was covered with good-luck
feathers.

"This bird is used to traffic,"
said the passenger.
"It once belonged to a racing driver.
Here you are — and good luck!"
        "Thank you, my friend. Thank you!"
cried Captain Castor.
        The parrot got on the bus
and looked around with a wicked eye.
"Okay, okay," it said,
"let's get this show on the road."

Captain Castor pulled out into the morning traffic. He was no longer afraid. The parrot had thousands of feathers, and they would all bring good luck.

The parrot hopped up and down on the hat.

"Get moving!" it screeched.

"We are moving," said Captain Castor.

"You could have fooled me," said the parrot.

"Come on! Put your foot down!"

The bus went faster,
but not fast enough for the parrot.
It had belonged to a racing driver.
It hungered for speed.
It thirsted for speed.
"Give it the gas!" it cried.

Captain Castor went as
fast as he could.
Shops rushed past.
The bus rocked from side to side.
Cars tooted their horns in alarm.
    "Slow down!" yelled the passengers.
"You'll have an accident!"
    "Don't worry," called Captain Castor.
He knew he was safe
with all those good-luck feathers.

The parrot hopped onto his jacket.
"Faster!" it screamed in his ear.
It swung on his gold earring.
"Faster, faster, Captain Castor!"
    The bus rocked over the hill
and down the other side.
It went so fast,
the wheels came off the road.
        "Stop!" yelled the passengers.

Captain Castor couldn't stop.
He had lost control.
The bus raced down the hill.
Into the park it went.
It bounced over a soccer field
and through a duck pond.
Then it stopped in the middle
of a flower garden.

The parrot lay on the floor,
yellow feathers everywhere.
"Disaster, Captain Castor!"
it screeched.

The passengers got out.
"We'll walk the rest of the way,"
they said.
The parrot got out, too.
"You call yourself a driver!"
it screamed.
"Look what you've done.
I don't need you.
I'm off to find a racing driver."
Captain Castor yelled back,
"You call yourself a good-luck parrot!

Look what you've done!
I don't need you, either.
I don't even need one of your feathers.
I can drive better
on my own!''

Captain Castor backed the bus
away from the flower garden.
He drove it out of the park.
His hands did not shake.
His feet did not shiver.

"A good driver doesn't need good
luck," he thought.

He stopped for more passengers.
As they got on, he sang,

"Never, never, no, not ever
will I need another feather."
    Then down the road he went, saying,
"That feather was a lot of nonsense!
Nothing but silly superstition!"

But he kept his fingers crossed
on the steering wheel, just to make sure.